DOCTOR WHO

VILLAINS & MONSTERS

D1503709

MAD LIBS®

by Rob Valois

PSS!
PRICE STERN SLOAN
An Imprint of Penguin Random House

PRICE STERN SLOAN
Penguin Young Readers Group
An Imprint of Penguin Random House LLC

Published in 2016 by Price Stern Sloan, an imprint of Penguin Random House LLC,
345 Hudson Street, New York, New York 10014. Printed in the USA.

ISBN 9780399539497
1 3 5 7 9 10 8 6 4 2

MAD LIBS

INSTRUCTIONS

MAD LIBS® is a game for people who don't like games! It can be played by one, two, three, four, or forty.

• RIDICULOUSLY SIMPLE DIRECTIONS

In this tablet you will find stories containing blank spaces where words are left out. One player, the READER, selects one of these stories. The READER does not tell anyone what the story is about. Instead, he/she asks the other players, the WRITERS, to give him/her words. These words are used to fill in the blank spaces in the story.

• TO PLAY

The READER asks each WRITER in turn to call out a word—an adjective or a noun or whatever the space calls for—and uses them to fill in the blank spaces in the story. The result is a MAD LIBS® game.

When the READER then reads the completed MAD LIBS® game to the other players, they will discover that they have written a story that is fantastic, screamingly funny, shocking, silly, crazy, or just plain dumb—depending upon which words each WRITER called out.

• EXAMPLE (*Before* and *After*)

"_____!" he said _____
  EXCLAMATION   ADVERB

as he jumped into his convertible _____ and
                                          NOUN

drove off with his _____ wife.
                          ADJECTIVE

"_____OUCH_____!" he said _____STUPIDLY_____
  EXCLAMATION   ADVERB

as he jumped into his convertible _____CAT_____ and
                                          NOUN

drove off with his _____BRAVE_____ wife.
                          ADJECTIVE

In case you have forgotten what adjectives, adverbs, nouns, and verbs are, here is a quick review:

An ADJECTIVE describes something or somebody. *Lumpy*, *soft*, *ugly*, *messy*, and *short* are adjectives.

An ADVERB tells how something is done. It modifies a verb and usually ends in "ly." *Modestly*, *stupidly*, *greedily*, and *carefully* are adverbs.

A NOUN is the name of a person, place, or thing. *Sidewalk*, *umbrella*, *bridle*, *bathtub*, and *nose* are nouns.

A VERB is an action word. *Run*, *pitch*, *jump*, and *swim* are verbs. Put the verbs in past tense if the directions say PAST TENSE. *Ran*, *pitched*, *jumped*, and *swam* are verbs in the past tense.

When we ask for A PLACE, we mean any sort of place: a country or city (*Spain*, *Cleveland*) or a room (*bathroom*, *kitchen*).

An EXCLAMATION or SILLY WORD is any sort of funny sound, gasp, grunt, or outcry, like *Wow!*, *Ouch!*, *Whomp!*, *Ick!*, and *Gadzooks!*

When we ask for specific words, like a NUMBER, a COLOR, an ANIMAL, or a PART OF THE BODY, we mean a word that is one of those things, like *seven*, *blue*, *horse*, or *head*.

When we ask for a PLURAL, it means more than one. For example, *cat* pluralized is *cats*.

MAD LIBS® is fun to play with friends, but you can also play it by yourself! To begin with, DO NOT look at the story on the page below. Fill in the blanks on this page with the words called for. Then, using the words you have selected, fill in the blank spaces in the story.

Now you've created your own hilarious MAD LIBS® game!

MISSY AND HER DOCTOR

NOUN _____

ADJECTIVE _____

NOUN _____

NUMBER _____

PLURAL NOUN _____

NOUN _____

NOUN _____

ADJECTIVE _____

PLURAL NOUN _____

NUMBER _____

NOUN _____

ADJECTIVE _____

NOUN _____

PERSON IN ROOM (FEMALE) _____

ADJECTIVE _____

MAD☺LIBS®
MISSY AND HER
DOCTOR

The Doctor and the Master: two sides of the same _____.
NOUN

One is good and the other deplorably _____. These two
ADJECTIVE

_____ Lords have known each other for nearly _____
NOUN   NUMBER

years, ever since they were both small _____ on the planet
PLURAL NOUN

_____. Although they have a shared _____, they
NOUN   NOUN

couldn't be any more _____. Over numerous centuries and
ADJECTIVE

through multiple _____, they've each died and regenerated
PLURAL NOUN

_____ times. Though the Twelfth Doctor thought that the
NUMBER

Master was gone for good, his old _____ once again returned.
NOUN

This time, the _____ Time Lord regenerated into a Time
ADJECTIVE

_____. The Master was now called _____.
NOUN   PERSON IN ROOM (FEMALE)

And although the Doctor didn't recognize her at first, he soon learned

that the Master was not only still alive but as _____ as ever.
ADJECTIVE

From DOCTOR WHO: VILLAINS AND MONSTERS MAD LIBS® • BBC, DOCTOR WHO
(word marks, logos and devices), TARDIS, DALEKS, CYBERMAN and K-9 (word marks and devices)
are trademarks of the British Broadcasting Corporation and are used under license. Published in 2016 by
Price Stern Sloan, an imprint of Penguin Random House LLC, 345 Hudson Street, New York, NY 10014.

MAD LIBS® is fun to play with friends, but you can also play it by yourself! To begin with, DO NOT look at the story on the page below. Fill in the blanks on this page with the words called for. Then, using the words you have selected, fill in the blank spaces in the story.

Now you've created your own hilarious MAD LIBS® game!

MEET THE DALEKS

NOUN _____

PLURAL NOUN _____

ADJECTIVE _____

A PLACE _____

ADJECTIVE _____

PLURAL NOUN _____

ADJECTVE _____

PLURAL NOUN _____

ADJECTIVE _____

PERSON IN ROOM _____

PLURAL NOUN _____

ADJECTIVE _____

NOUN _____

ADVERB _____

ADJECTIVE _____

EXCLAMATION _____

PLURAL NOUN _____

MAD LIBS®

MEET THE DALEKS

If there is one _____ that is associated with the Doctor, more
                        NOUN

than any of his other foes, it's the depraved _____ known
                                              PLURAL NOUN

as the Daleks. The Doctor has chased these terrible and _____
                                                        ADJECTIVE

creatures from one corner of (the) _____ to the other, and
                                   A PLACE

through the _____ expanse of the _____. These
            ADJECTIVE   PLURAL NOUN

_____ villains had their _____ stripped away and
ADJECTIVE   PLURAL NOUN

were left with only _____ rage and a singular hatred toward
                    ADJECTIVE

_____. These twisted _____ have each been
PERSON IN ROOM   PLURAL NOUN

encased in a/an _____ shell of solid, metallic _____
                ADJECTIVE   NOUN

that is _____ indestructible. The Daleks' _____
        ADVERB   ADJECTIVE

battle cry of "_____!" can often be heard across
               EXCLAMATION

many battlefields throughout the universe as they vaporize any

_____ that get in their way.
PLURAL NOUN

From DOCTOR WHO: VILLAINS AND MONSTERS MAD LIBS® • BBC, DOCTOR WHO
(word marks, logos and devices), TARDIS, DALEKS, CYBERMAN and K-9 (word marks and devices)
are trademarks of the British Broadcasting Corporation and are used under license. Published in 2016 by
Price Stern Sloan, an imprint of Penguin Random House LLC, 345 Hudson Street, New York, NY 10014.

MAD LIBS® is fun to play with friends, but you can also play it by yourself! To begin with, DO NOT look at the story on the page below. Fill in the blanks on this page with the words called for. Then, using the words you have selected, fill in the blank spaces in the story.

Now you've created your own hilarious MAD LIBS® game!

TICKTOCK

NOUN _____

ADJECTIVE _____

A PLACE _____

ADVERB _____

NOUN _____

PART OF THE BODY _____

NOUN _____

A PLACE _____

NOUN _____

ADJECTIVE _____

PLURAL NOUN _____

ADVERB _____

MAD LIBS

TICKTOCK

"Do you hear that sound?" the Doctor asked Clara. They were sitting

on an old _____ in the center of the _____ chamber.
NOUN   ADJECTIVE

The TARDIS had brought them to (the) _____, but the Doctor
                                          A PLACE

couldn't figure out why. "Which sound?" she replied _____,
                                                         ADVERB

her eyes scanning the _____ for something out of place. "All
                            NOUN

I can hear are the rumblings of my own _____ and the sound
                                          PART OF THE BODY

from that old wind-up _____ hanging on the wall." "The one
                            NOUN

with the hands that have stopped moving?" he asked, pointing to the

wall. "And you should have eaten something from (the) _____
                                                           A PLACE

back when we stopped there. The fermented _____ looked
                                                 NOUN

quite intriguing." "That _____ sound is getting closer," Clara
                              ADJECTIVE

said. "I think it's coming from behind us." "That's what I'm afraid of,"

said the Doctor. "So what do we do?" Clara asked, turning her head

to see several clockwork _____ lumbering _____
                               PLURAL NOUN   ADVERB

toward her and the Doctor. "I would suggest running," the Doctor

replied.

From DOCTOR WHO: VILLAINS AND MONSTERS MAD LIBS® • BBC, DOCTOR WHO
(word marks, logos and devices), TARDIS, DALEKS, CYBERMAN and K-9 (word marks and devices)
are trademarks of the British Broadcasting Corporation and are used under license. Published in 2016 by
Price Stern Sloan, an imprint of Penguin Random House LLC, 345 Hudson Street, New York, NY 10014.

MAD LIBS® is fun to play with friends, but you can also play it by yourself! To begin with, DO NOT look at the story on the page below. Fill in the blanks on this page with the words called for. Then, using the words you have selected, fill in the blank spaces in the story.

Now you've created your own hilarious MAD LIBS® game!

HERE COME THE DRUMS

ADJECTIVE _____

NOUN _____

ADJECTIVE _____

ADJECTIVE _____

PERSON IN ROOM _____

NOUN _____

PERSON IN ROOM (FEMALE) _____

PERSON IN ROOM (MALE) _____

NOUN _____

CELEBRITY _____

A PLACE _____

ADJECTIVE _____

MAD LIBS®

HERE COME THE DRUMS

The Tenth Doctor encountered the _____ Time Lord, the
ADJECTIVE

Master, for the first time after landing his _____ on a/an
NOUN

_____ planet perched at the end of both the universe and
ADJECTIVE

time itself. Having regenerated into a/an _____ scientist
ADJECTIVE

named Professor _____, the Master was unrecognizable
PERSON IN ROOM

to the Doctor. Catching the Doctor off guard, the Master stole the

Tenth Doctor's _____ and left him stranded—but not
NOUN

before regenerating one more time. The Doctor and his companions,

_____ and Captain _____, used a/an
PERSON IN ROOM (FEMALE)   PERSON IN ROOM (MALE)

_____ manipulator to return to Earth. They arrived to find
NOUN

that the regenerated Master had assumed the name _____
CELEBRITY

and had become the Prime Minister of (the) _____. With his
A PLACE

newfound power and status, it seemed that the Master was now more

powerful and _____ than even the Doctor himself.
ADJECTIVE

From DOCTOR WHO: VILLAINS AND MONSTERS MAD LIBS® • BBC, DOCTOR WHO
(word marks, logos and devices), TARDIS, DALEKS, CYBERMAN and K-9 (word marks and devices)
are trademarks of the British Broadcasting Corporation and are used under license. Published in 2016 by
Price Stern Sloan, an imprint of Penguin Random House LLC, 345 Hudson Street, New York, NY 10014.

MAD LIBS® is fun to play with friends, but you can also play it by yourself! To begin with, DO NOT look at the story on the page below. Fill in the blanks on this page with the words called for. Then, using the words you have selected, fill in the blank spaces in the story.

Now you've created your own hilarious MAD LIBS® game!

THE OOD ONE OUT

NOUN _____

ADJECTIVE _____

PLURAL NOUN _____

ADJECTIVE _____

NUMBER _____

PLURAL NOUN _____

PLURAL NOUN _____

ADJECTIVE _____

ADJECTIVE _____

NOUN _____

ADJECTIVE _____

PART OF THE BODY _____

VERB _____

PLURAL NOUN _____

MAD LIBS

THE OOD ONE OUT

The Ood, also known as the _____-kind, are a/an
                                   NOUN

_____ race of telepathic _____. These naturally
   ADJECTIVE   PLURAL NOUN

_____ creatures have _____ tentacles hanging from
   ADJECTIVE   NUMBER

their faces, making them resemble humanoid _____. Each
                                               PLURAL NOUN

Ood has two _____, one of which they hold in their hand,
               PLURAL NOUN

making them extremely _____. When the Doctor first met
                          ADJECTIVE

them, the Ood appeared to be _____ and quite aggressive—
                                 ADJECTIVE

but it turned out that they had been enslaved by an ancient evil

known as the _____. Once the evil telepathic connection
                 NOUN

was broken, the Ood returned to their usual calm and _____
                                                         ADJECTIVE

selves. It was easy to tell when an Ood was being controlled, because

its _____ would glow fiery red—that was always a sure sign
    PART OF THE BODY

to _____. After being freed, the Ood befriended the Doctor
    VERB

and often gave him _____ when he was in danger.
                       PLURAL NOUN

MAD LIBS® is fun to play with friends, but you can also play it by yourself! To begin with, DO NOT look at the story on the page below. Fill in the blanks on this page with the words called for. Then, using the words you have selected, fill in the blank spaces in the story.

Now you've created your own hilarious MAD LIBS® game!

YOU BLINKED

ADVERB _____

ADJECTIVE _____

PLURAL NOUN _____

ADVERB _____

ADJECTIVE _____

NOUN _____

A PLACE _____

PLURAL NOUN _____

ADJECTIVE _____

NOUN _____

ADJECTIVE _____

PLURAL NOUN _____

PLURAL NOUN _____

ADJECTIVE _____

PART OF THE BODY _____

MAD LIBS®

YOU BLINKED

Clara trod _____ along the _____ path. She loved
         ADVERB   ADJECTIVE

to explore new _____, and this one was no different. The
              PLURAL NOUN

Doctor strolled a bit more _____ behind her. The TARDIS
                     ADVERB

was parked just beyond a statue of a/an _____ and noble
                                  ADJECTIVE

_____. The Doctor was also enjoying their final evening in
   NOUN

the ancient city of (the) _____. He especially liked the old
                     A PLACE

stone _____ and the _____ statues that lined
       PLURAL NOUN   ADJECTIVE

the walkways. The light from Clara's _____ flickered in the
                            NOUN

_____ evening breeze, leaving the Doctor momentarily in
   ADJECTIVE

the dark. When the light returned, the Doctor noticed that the stone

_____ had moved—they were closing in on them. "Clara,"
   PLURAL NOUN

he called out, "whatever you do, don't close your _____."
                               PLURAL NOUN

As she turned to face him, her torch flickered in the wind one last

time—revealing a/an _____ Weeping Angel's clawed hand
              ADJECTIVE

just inches from her _____.
             PART OF THE BODY

MAD LIBS® is fun to play with friends, but you can also play it by yourself! To begin with, DO NOT look at the story on the page below. Fill in the blanks on this page with the words called for. Then, using the words you have selected, fill in the blank spaces in the story.

Now you've created your own hilarious MAD LIBS® game!

THE GREAT INTELLIGENCE

ADJECTIVE _____

NOUN _____

NUMBER _____

PLURAL NOUN _____

PLURAL NOUN _____

A PLACE _____

ADJECTIVE _____

PLURAL NOUN _____

PLURAL NOUN _____

ADJECTIVE _____

NOUN _____

ADJECTIVE _____

PERSON IN ROOM (FEMALE) _____

NOUN _____

MAD LIBS
THE GREAT
INTELLIGENCE

The _____ Intelligence was a malevolent _____ that
    ADJECTIVE   NOUN

lacked any true form and existed throughout _____ dimensions.
                                                     NUMBER

This incorporeal being imprinted its desires on unsuspecting

_____. The Doctor had encountered it many times. In
PLURAL NOUN

1935, the Second Doctor found that it was controlling a group of

robotic abominable snow-_____ deep in the mountains of
                                             PLURAL NOUN

(the) _____. After several _____ confrontations with
       A PLACE   ADJECTIVE

the Doctor, the Intelligence enlisted the Whisper _____ to
                                                 PLURAL NOUN

kidnap the Doctor's _____ and lead him to Trenzalore.
                              PLURAL NOUN

The Intelligence had planned its _____ revenge—to enter
                                    ADJECTIVE

the Doctor's _____-stream and undo all the _____
               NOUN   ADJECTIVE

things he'd done in his life. However, the Intelligence didn't expect that

_____ would follow it through the wound and save
PERSON IN ROOM (FEMALE)

the Doctor, preventing any damage to his _____.
                                                      NOUN

From DOCTOR WHO: VILLAINS AND MONSTERS MAD LIBS® • BBC, DOCTOR WHO
(word marks, logos and devices), TARDIS, DALEKS, CYBERMAN and K-9 (word marks and devices)
are trademarks of the British Broadcasting Corporation and are used under license. Published in 2016 by
Price Stern Sloan, an imprint of Penguin Random House LLC, 345 Hudson Street, New York, NY 10014.

MAD LIBS® is fun to play with friends, but you can also play it by yourself! To begin with, DO NOT look at the story on the page below. Fill in the blanks on this page with the words called for. Then, using the words you have selected, fill in the blank spaces in the story.

Now you've created your own hilarious MAD LIBS® game!

THE UPGRADE

EXCLAMATION _____

PLURAL NOUN _____

NOUN _____

NUMBER _____

ADJECTIVE _____

PLURAL NOUN _____

ADVERB _____

NOUN _____

ADJECTIVE _____

ARTICLE OF CLOTHING _____

ADJECTIVE _____

ADJECTIVE _____

NUMBER _____

PLURAL NOUN _____

ADJECTIVE _____

VERB ENDING IN "ING" _____

PLURAL NOUN _____

MAD LIBS

THE UPGRADE

"_____!" you scream as the now familiar sound of

   EXCLAMATION

metallic _____ clang and stomp, and the frightening

     PLURAL NOUN

_____-men make their way toward you. It's been _____

  NOUN   NUMBER

weeks since these _____, metal men arrived, and they've

           ADJECTIVE

already upgraded most of the _____. Even though there's

                PLURAL NOUN

not much chance of survival, you _____ duck behind a rusty

                   ADVERB

old _____. You've heard rumors of a/an _____ man

    NOUN   ADJECTIVE

in a blue _____ who is coming to save you—then

       ARTICLE OF CLOTHING

save the whole _____ planet. They say that the Doctor can

         ADJECTIVE

stop these _____ monsters, and you hope it's true because

      ADJECTIVE

there are _____ of them heading in your direction. The sound

     NUMBER

of the metallic _____ marching in unison gets louder until

        PLURAL NOUN

it eventually stops. And although you can't see the Doctor through the

_____ smoke, you can hear the _____ sound

 ADJECTIVE   VERB ENDING IN "ING"

of something sonic in the distance and of _____ crashing

                         PLURAL NOUN

to the ground.

From DOCTOR WHO: VILLAINS AND MONSTERS MAD LIBS® • BBC, DOCTOR WHO
(word marks, logos and devices), TARDIS, DALEKS, CYBERMAN and K-9 (word marks and devices)
are trademarks of the British Broadcasting Corporation and are used under license. Published in 2016 by
Price Stern Sloan, an imprint of Penguin Random House LLC, 345 Hudson Street, New York, NY 10014.

MAD LIBS® is fun to play with friends, but you can also play it by yourself! To begin with, DO NOT look at the story on the page below. Fill in the blanks on this page with the words called for. Then, using the words you have selected, fill in the blank spaces in the story.

Now you've created your own hilarious MAD LIBS® game!

THE ORIGINAL EARTHLINGS

PLURAL NOUN _____

NOUN _____

ADJECTIVE _____

NOUN _____

NUMBER _____

ADJECTIVE _____

PLURAL NOUN _____

ADJECTIVE _____

NOUN _____

NOUN _____

PERSON IN ROOM (FEMALE) _____

MAD LIBS®
THE ORIGINAL
EARTHLINGS

Believe it or not, _____ were not the original inhabitants
                        PLURAL NOUN

of Earth. Long before the human race first took form, a race of

_____-like creatures known as the Silurians roamed a molten
      NOUN

and _____ planet. These reptilian beings created a vast
        ADJECTIVE

_____ that thrived for over _____ years. However,
      NOUN   NUMBER

because they needed to live in a very _____ environment,
                                          ADJECTIVE

they went into hibernation as the Earth's _____ began
                                              PLURAL NOUN

to cool. Centuries passed, and humans evolved to become the most

_____ of all life on Earth. It wasn't until the heat from a
      ADJECTIVE

nuclear _____ awoke them that the Third Doctor had to be
            NOUN

called in to stop the Silurians from trying to reclaim their place at the

top of the _____ chain. Years later, a Silurian named Madame
                NOUN

_____ became a close companion to the Eleventh
PERSON IN ROOM (FEMALE)

Doctor.

MAD LIBS® is fun to play with friends, but you can also play it by yourself! To begin with, DO NOT look at the story on the page below. Fill in the blanks on this page with the words called for. Then, using the words you have selected, fill in the blank spaces in the story.

Now you've created your own hilarious MAD LIBS® game!

THE MYSTERIOUS SHAKRI

NOUN _____

PLURAL NOUN _____

PLURAL NOUN _____

ADJECTIVE _____

ADJECTIVE _____

PLURAL NOUN _____

ADJECTIVE _____

NOUN _____

PLURAL NOUN _____

NOUN _____

ADJECTIVE _____

A PLACE _____

MAD LIBS®
THE MYSTERIOUS SHAKRI

When the Doctor was a young boy on the planet _____, the
NOUN

children were told stories about a race of frightening _____
PLURAL NOUN

known only as the Shakri. They were _____ that would
PLURAL NOUN

come get children if they were _____ and didn't behave.
ADJECTIVE

As he grew older, the Doctor assumed it was nothing more than

a/an _____ myth—something to keep the _____
ADJECTIVE   PLURAL NOUN

of Gallifrey in their place. Then one day, he realized that the

_____ Shakri do exist and that they planned to destroy
ADJECTIVE

every _____ on Earth. These mysterious creatures claim to
NOUN

exist in all _____ in time, but also in none. They follow
PLURAL NOUN

a belief known as the Tally, or _____ Day, that drove them
NOUN

to eliminate races that could be considered _____. And they
ADJECTIVE

decided that humanity must be eliminated before they could colonize

(the) _____.
A PLACE

From DOCTOR WHO: VILLAINS AND MONSTERS MAD LIBS® • BBC, DOCTOR WHO
(word marks, logos and devices), TARDIS, DALEKS, CYBERMAN and K-9 (word marks and devices)
are trademarks of the British Broadcasting Corporation and are used under license. Published in 2016 by
Price Stern Sloan, an imprint of Penguin Random House LLC, 345 Hudson Street, New York, NY 10014.

MAD LIBS® is fun to play with friends, but you can also play it by yourself! To begin with, DO NOT look at the story on the page below. Fill in the blanks on this page with the words called for. Then, using the words you have selected, fill in the blank spaces in the story.

Now you've created your own hilarious MAD LIBS® game!

THEY CAME FROM SKARO

ADJECTIVE _____

A PLACE _____

PLURAL NOUN _____

ADJECTIVE _____

NOUN _____

ADJECTIVE _____

PLURAL NOUN _____

PLURAL NOUN _____

ADJECTIVE _____

NOUN _____

ADJECTIVE _____

ADJECTIVE _____

PLURAL NOUN _____

MAD LIBS®
THEY CAME FROM SKARO

It's difficult to recall a time when the _____ Daleks didn't

ADJECTIVE

terrorize (the) _____. These destructive armored _____

A PLACE   PLURAL NOUN

were first created on the planet Skaro by a/an _____ scientist

ADJECTIVE

called Davros. He was the senior _____ of the Kaled people,

NOUN

who had been suffering from an extended and _____

ADJECTIVE

war with the neighboring _____ of Thals. The Kaleds

PLURAL NOUN

had become mutated by biological and nuclear _____.

PLURAL NOUN

Davros accelerated this horrific process to create a race of heartless,

_____ killers that he placed in armored tank-like shells. He

ADJECTIVE

believed that he had created the perfect _____ to use against

NOUN

his enemies. After years of fighting the Daleks, the Doctor learned of

their one weakness. As a/an _____ child, Davros was rescued

ADJECTIVE

by the Twelfth Doctor. Because of this, Davros unknowingly instilled

in the Daleks one of the _____ traits of the Doctor—the

ADJECTIVE

concept of _____.

PLURAL NOUN

MAD LIBS® is fun to play with friends, but you can also play it by yourself! To begin with, DO NOT look at the story on the page below. Fill in the blanks on this page with the words called for. Then, using the words you have selected, fill in the blank spaces in the story.

Now you've created your own hilarious MAD LIBS® game!

FEAR THE SILENCE

NOUN _____

ADJECTIVE _____

PART OF THE BODY _____

PLURAL NOUN _____

NOUN _____

ADJECTIVE _____

NOUN _____

ADJECTIVE _____

COLOR _____

PART OF THE BODY (PLURAL) _____

NOUN _____

ADVERB _____

NOUN _____

NUMBER _____

PLURAL NOUN _____

MAD⊙LIBS®

FEAR THE SILENCE

Imagine a/an _____ so powerful and so _____
NOUN   ADJECTIVE

that after you look away, you have no memory of ever having seen

it. Its whole existence is completely wiped from your _____
PART OF THE BODY

without a trace. The Silence are a race of genetically engineered

_____ who use hypnotic suggestion, or _____
PLURAL NOUN   NOUN

control, to manipulate other species into doing their _____
ADJECTIVE

bidding. They could convince any person to destroy his or her own

best _____ without even realizing they're doing it. These
NOUN

_____ creatures have a ghostly _____ appearance
ADJECTIVE   COLOR

and no _____. They have been lurking on Earth
PART OF THE BODY (PLURAL)

since the early days of _____-kind. If you ever encounter one,
NOUN

_____ grab a/an _____ and make a mark on your
ADVERB   NOUN

skin. You won't remember doing it, but you'll soon start to notice the

one, two, or even _____ marks on your body. You can then only
NUMBER

guess at what the horrific _____ asked you to do.
PLURAL NOUN

MAD LIBS® is fun to play with friends, but you can also play it by yourself! To begin with, DO NOT look at the story on the page below. Fill in the blanks on this page with the words called for. Then, using the words you have selected, fill in the blank spaces in the story.

Now you've created your own hilarious MAD LIBS® game!

COMPANION DOWN

ADJECTIVE _____

NOUN _____

A PLACE _____

NOUN _____

ADJECTIVE _____

NUMBER _____

ADJECTIVE _____

ADVERB _____

NOUN _____

NOUN _____

NUMBER _____

PERSON IN ROOM (MALE) _____

NOUN _____

PLURAL NOUN _____

ADJECTIVE _____

CELEBRITY _____

MAD LIBS

COMPANION DOWN

Not only was this the first time you'd been aboard a/an _____
ADJECTIVE

space- _____, but it was also the first time you'd been away from
NOUN

(the) _____ . It should have been an exciting _____,
A PLACE   NOUN

but instead it is turning out to be _____ and frightening.
                                    ADJECTIVE

For _____ days you fled the _____ creatures—each
      NUMBER   ADJECTIVE

time you _____ thought you were safe, they found your
          ADVERB

secret _____ . Then, the doors to the _____ closed
        NOUN   NOUN

before you could reach them. It's been nearly _____ hours since
                                               NUMBER

you last saw the evil _____, but you know he's close.
                       PERSON IN ROOM (MALE)

And although the Doctor promised to keep you safe, he is nowhere

to be seen. You keep expecting to hear the familiar sound of the

_____ materializing behind you, but all your cries for help
NOUN

have gone unanswered. You're going to have to take _____
                                                    PLURAL NOUN

into your own hands and confront this _____ beast without
                                       ADJECTIVE

the Doctor's help. _____ help us all.
                    CELEBRITY

MAD LIBS® is fun to play with friends, but you can also play it by yourself! To begin with, DO NOT look at the story on the page below. Fill in the blanks on this page with the words called for. Then, using the words you have selected, fill in the blank spaces in the story.

Now you've created your own hilarious MAD LIBS® game!

MARS ATTACKS

PERSON IN ROOM _____

ADJECTIVE _____

PLURAL NOUN _____

ADJECTIVE _____

PLURAL NOUN _____

ADJECTIVE _____

PLURAL NOUN _____

ADJECTIVE _____

COLOR _____

ADJECTIVE _____

PLURAL NOUN _____

ADJECTIVE _____

A PLACE _____

NUMBER _____

ADJECTIVE _____

PLURAL NOUN _____

MAD LIBS

MARS ATTACKS

Rising from the ice and snow, you can see Grand Marshal

_____ from the _____ planet Mars. This militaristic
PERSON IN ROOM   ADJECTIVE

creature is from a race known as the Ice _____, a/an
                                        PLURAL NOUN

_____ and noble breed that made their home on ancient
ADJECTIVE

Mars. These cold-blooded _____ thrived on the planet's
                                PLURAL NOUN

icy and _____ terrain and built massive cities out of frozen
             ADJECTIVE

_____. They have _____ armor, but below lies
PLURAL NOUN   ADJECTIVE

_____ reptilian skin, a/an _____ body, and fiery red
COLOR   ADJECTIVE

_____. These soldiers are as fierce as they are _____
PLURAL NOUN   ADJECTIVE

and equally feared and respected throughout (the) _____.
                                            A PLACE

After _____ generations, the Martian atmosphere has thinned,
       NUMBER

and the planet's temperature is rising. The creatures need to find a

new home—someplace cold and _____. Some have headed
                                ADJECTIVE

to Earth to build a new life on the frozen _____ of the
                                     PLURAL NOUN

planet's poles.

From DOCTOR WHO: VILLAINS AND MONSTERS MAD LIBS® • BBC, DOCTOR WHO
(word marks, logos and devices), TARDIS, DALEKS, CYBERMAN and K-9 (word marks and devices)
are trademarks of the British Broadcasting Corporation and are used under license. Published in 2016 by
Price Stern Sloan, an imprint of Penguin Random House LLC, 345 Hudson Street, New York, NY 10014.

MAD LIBS® is fun to play with friends, but you can also play it by yourself! To begin with, DO NOT look at the story on the page below. Fill in the blanks on this page with the words called for. Then, using the words you have selected, fill in the blank spaces in the story.

Now you've created your own hilarious MAD LIBS® game!

A CYBER HISTORY

PLURAL NOUN _____

NUMBER _____

ADJECTIVE _____

PERSON IN ROOM _____

A PLACE _____

NUMBER _____

NOUN _____

PLURAL NOUN _____

PART OF THE BODY _____

ADJECTIVE _____

PLURAL NOUN _____

ADJECTIVE _____

MAD LIBS

A CYBER HISTORY

The Cyber-_____ have been enemies of the Doctor for

       PLURAL NOUN

more than _____ years. These _____ and emotionless

    NUMBER   ADJECTIVE

beings have seen many defeats at the hands of _____. The

                        PERSON IN ROOM

original Cybermen were created on Earth's twin planet named (the)

_____. The planet had drifted away to the edge of space, and

  A PLACE

the Cybermen planned to destroy Earth and have their world take its

place. It would take _____ incarnations of the Doctor to finally

                 NUMBER

defeat the Cybermen. Years later, a new breed of Cybermen would

emerge from a parallel _____. Like the previous version, these

                   NOUN

metal _____ believed that the human _____ was

     PLURAL NOUN   PART OF THE BODY

weak and _____ and needed to be upgraded. Regardless of

        ADJECTIVE

their origins, the Cybermen have always been a threat to Earth and

to _____ everywhere. That's what makes them such a/an

    PLURAL NOUN

_____ foe for the Doctor.

  ADJECTIVE

From DOCTOR WHO: VILLAINS AND MONSTERS MAD LIBS® • BBC, DOCTOR WHO
(word marks, logos and devices), TARDIS, DALEKS, CYBERMAN and K-9 (word marks and devices)
are trademarks of the British Broadcasting Corporation and are used under license. Published in 2016 by
Price Stern Sloan, an imprint of Penguin Random House LLC, 345 Hudson Street, New York, NY 10014.

MAD LIBS® is fun to play with friends, but you can also play it by yourself! To begin with, DO NOT look at the story on the page below. Fill in the blanks on this page with the words called for. Then, using the words you have selected, fill in the blank spaces in the story.

Now you've created your own hilarious MAD LIBS® game!

HOLD ON TO YOUR HEAD

PLURAL NOUN _____

PERSON IN ROOM (FEMALE) _____

PART OF THE BODY (PLURAL) _____

ADJECTIVE _____

ADJECTIVE _____

PLURAL NOUN _____

PART OF THE BODY (PLURAL) _____

ADVERB _____

PLURAL NOUN _____

VERB _____

ADJECTIVE _____

ADVERB _____

MAD LIBS®
HOLD ON TO YOUR HEAD

The Headless _____ were a group of monks recruited
                    PLURAL NOUN

by Madame _____ to help the Silence defeat the
              PERSON IN ROOM (FEMALE)

Doctor. They were fierce fighters and could fire energy blasts from

their _____. They could also concentrate their
       PART OF THE BODY (PLURAL)

_____ energy through the swords that all _____
   ADJECTIVE   ADJECTIVE

members of their order carried. These _____ believed in
                                          PLURAL NOUN

listening to their _____ instead of their minds—
                    PART OF THE BODY (PLURAL)

which is why they beheaded themselves. Because of this, they

_____ believed that they couldn't be fooled, surprised, or even
   ADVERB

feel _____. Despite having no heads, these villains were
        PLURAL NOUN

able to _____. One of the most _____ things about
           VERB   ADJECTIVE

them was their chanting. Once an opponent heard it, they knew they

needed to run or be _____ smote.
                        ADVERB

MAD LIBS® is fun to play with friends, but you can also play it by yourself! To begin with, DO NOT look at the story on the page below. Fill in the blanks on this page with the words called for. Then, using the words you have selected, fill in the blank spaces in the story.

Now you've created your own hilarious MAD LIBS® game!

THE ZYGON FILES

PART OF THE BODY (PLURAL) _____

NOUN _____

ADJECTIVE _____

ADVERB _____

ADJECTIVE _____

CELEBRITY _____

PERSON IN ROOM _____

COLOR _____

NOUN _____

PLURAL NOUN _____

NOUN _____

NOUN _____

COLOR _____

ADJECTIVE _____

PART OF THE BODY _____

ADJECTIVE _____

PLURAL NOUN _____

MAD LIBS®

THE ZYGON FILES

Don't believe what your _____ tell you, because that
PART OF THE BODY (PLURAL)

_____ in front of you might not be what you think it is. That
NOUN

_____ person sitting across from you may actually be a Zygon
ADJECTIVE

in disguise, ready to _____ attack at any moment. These
ADVERB

_____ foes of _____ can transform themselves to
ADJECTIVE   CELEBRITY

look like anyone they want. Could it be that _____ is really a/an
PERSON IN ROOM

_____-skinned alien from the planet _____? Maybe
COLOR   NOUN

the person who served you your _____ this morning or
PLURAL NOUN

the person who filled up your _____ is really a creature
NOUN

from another world. These _____-headed beings have
NOUN

_____ skin, and _____ suckers cover them from
COLOR   ADJECTIVE

_____ to foot. It's no surprise that these _____
PART OF THE BODY   ADJECTIVE

creatures like to transform into _____!
PLURAL NOUN

From DOCTOR WHO: VILLAINS AND MONSTERS MAD LIBS® • BBC, DOCTOR WHO
(word marks, logos and devices), TARDIS, DALEKS, CYBERMAN and K-9 (word marks and devices)
are trademarks of the British Broadcasting Corporation and are used under license. Published in 2016 by
Price Stern Sloan, an imprint of Penguin Random House LLC, 345 Hudson Street, New York, NY 10014.

MAD LIBS® is fun to play with friends, but you can also play it by yourself! To begin with, DO NOT look at the story on the page below. Fill in the blanks on this page with the words called for. Then, using the words you have selected, fill in the blank spaces in the story.

Now you've created your own hilarious MAD LIBS® game!

BEWARE THE PLASTIC MEN

ADVERB _____

NOUN _____

PLURAL NOUN _____

ADJECTIVE _____

NOUN _____

ADJECTIVE _____

ADVERB _____

ADJECTIVE _____

NOUN _____

COLOR _____

NUMBER _____

PLURAL NOUN _____

ADJECTIVE _____

NOUN _____

PLURAL NOUN _____

MAD LIBS®
BEWARE THE PLASTIC MEN

Clara and the Doctor _____ made their way through an
                            ADVERB
old abandoned _____ store. Aisles and aisles of broken
                    NOUN
toys, _____, and mannequins were spread out in every
        PLURAL NOUN
direction. Something _____ caught Clara's eye. "Hey, did
                            ADJECTIVE
that plastic _____ over there just move?" she asked. "Don't be
                NOUN
_____," the Doctor replied _____. "Human beings
   ADJECTIVE   ADVERB
will believe everything they see—especially the _____ ones.
                                                    ADJECTIVE
Plastic can't move. Not on its own. Unless it can. Or unless someone
or something is making it move." The Doctor pulled out his sonic
_____ and took a reading. The _____ glow illuminated
   NOUN   COLOR
the room enough for Clara to see _____ mannequins headed their
                                        NUMBER
way. "What are these things?" she asked. "Autons," replied the Doctor.
"_____ made out of plastic." "Are they _____?" Clara
   PLURAL NOUN   ADJECTIVE
asked, grabbing a/an _____ from a shelf to protect herself.
                            NOUN
"No," said the Doctor. "What you really need to worry about are the
nasty _____ that are controlling them . . ."
        PLURAL NOUN

From DOCTOR WHO: VILLAINS AND MONSTERS MAD LIBS® • BBC, DOCTOR WHO
(word marks, logos and devices), TARDIS, DALEKS, CYBERMAN and K-9 (word marks and devices)
are trademarks of the British Broadcasting Corporation and are used under license. Published in 2016 by
Price Stern Sloan, an imprint of Penguin Random House LLC, 345 Hudson Street, New York, NY 10014.

MAD LIBS® is fun to play with friends, but you can also play it by yourself! To begin with, DO NOT look at the story on the page below. Fill in the blanks on this page with the words called for. Then, using the words you have selected, fill in the blank spaces in the story.

Now you've created your own hilarious MAD LIBS® game!

JUDOON PLATOON

ANIMAL _____

ADJECTIVE _____

NOUN _____

ADVERB _____

ADJECTIVE _____

PLURAL NOUN _____

ADJECTIVE _____

A PLACE _____

PLURAL NOUN _____

NOUN _____

PERSON IN ROOM (FEMALE) _____

NOUN _____

MAD LIBS®

JUDOON PLATOON

The _____-headed Judoon are known throughout the universe
       ANIMAL

as some of the most _____ police officers and mercenary
                    ADJECTIVE

soldiers. They've been hired by all sorts of organizations, including the

_____ Proclamation. They are _____ able to carry
    NOUN   ADVERB

out tasks with great dedication, but often dispense _____
                                                   ADJECTIVE

justice—or even execution—without much thought. Although these

single-minded _____ are extremely methodical, the Doctor
              PLURAL NOUN

has noted that they can be a bit _____, and their actions are
                                ADJECTIVE

easy to predict. This is how he was able to outsmart them at (the)

_____ when they were searching for an alien in a hospital
   A PLACE

full of _____. With one kiss he was able to transfer a small
        PLURAL NOUN

amount of his non-_____ DNA to _____
                   NOUN   PERSON IN ROOM (FEMALE)

and confuse the Judoon into thinking she was the _____.
                                                 NOUN

From DOCTOR WHO: VILLAINS AND MONSTERS MAD LIBS® • BBC, DOCTOR WHO
(word marks, logos and devices), TARDIS, DALEKS, CYBERMAN and K-9 (word marks and devices)
are trademarks of the British Broadcasting Corporation and are used under license. Published in 2016 by
Price Stern Sloan, an imprint of Penguin Random House LLC, 345 Hudson Street, New York, NY 10014.

MAD LIBS® is fun to play with friends, but you can also play it by yourself! To begin with, DO NOT look at the story on the page below. Fill in the blanks on this page with the words called for. Then, using the words you have selected, fill in the blank spaces in the story.

Now you've created your own hilarious MAD LIBS® game!

GET TO KNOW A SONTARAN

PLURAL NOUN _____

A PLACE _____

ADJECTIVE _____

PLURAL NOUN _____

NOUN _____

ADJECTIVE _____

TYPE OF FOOD (PLURAL) _____

PLURAL NOUN _____

VERB _____

NUMBER _____

VERB ENDING IN "ING" _____

PLURAL NOUN _____

NOUN _____

NUMBER _____

There are many races of militaristic _____ throughout
PLURAL NOUN

(the) _____. However, the Sontarans are some of the most
A PLACE

ruthless and _____ soldiers that the Doctor has encountered
ADJECTIVE

during his travels. This race of clone _____ live by a strict
PLURAL NOUN

code of war, and pledge to live and die by the _____. These
NOUN

short and _____ beings are often described as looking like
ADJECTIVE

_____ crossed with _____. The Sontarans
TYPE OF FOOD (PLURAL)   PLURAL NOUN

are bred with only one purpose—to _____. Clones enter the
VERB

Sontaran army when they are only _____ years old. They are
NUMBER

born with the knowledge of many _____ techniques,
VERB ENDING IN "ING"

allowing them to defeat any _____, even at an early age.
PLURAL NOUN

They are not known to back down from a/an _____—even if
NOUN

they are outnumbered _____ to one.
NUMBER

MAD LIBS® is fun to play with friends, but you can also play it by yourself! To begin with, DO NOT look at the story on the page below. Fill in the blanks on this page with the words called for. Then, using the words you have selected, fill in the blank spaces in the story.

Now you've created your own hilarious MAD LIBS® game!

RETURN OF THE DALEKS

PLURAL NOUN _____

NOUN _____

PLURAL NOUN _____

ADJECTIVE _____

NOUN _____

ADJECTIVE _____

ADVERB _____

NOUN _____

NOUN _____

ADJECTIVE _____

PLURAL NOUN _____

NUMBER _____

MAD LIBS®
RETURN OF THE DALEKS

They say that all good _____ come to an end. Perhaps
                            PLURAL NOUN

that's why the Daleks never seem to go away. They lack even the tiniest

_____ of goodness and only wish to cause pain and bring
      NOUN

destruction to all _____ throughout the universe. Every
                         PLURAL NOUN

time the Doctor thinks he's finally vanquished these _____
                                                          ADJECTIVE

foes and eliminated them from every corner of the _____,
                                                        NOUN

they come back even more _____ than before. That's why the
                              ADJECTIVE

Doctor was _____ willing to sacrifice everything to defeat the
                ADVERB

Daleks during the _____ War, including destroying his own
                        NOUN

home planet of _____ and causing the extinction of all Time
                     NOUN

Lords. Imagine never being free from the _____ attacks from
                                               ADJECTIVE

these destructive _____. That's what the Doctor has been
                      PLURAL NOUN

dealing with for over _____ years.
                          NUMBER

Download Mad Libs today!

Join the millions of Mad [...]
wacky and wonderful stories o[...]

[...]et, New York, NY 10014.
[...]in 2016 by